HODDER
Wayland

an imprint of Hodder Children's Books

Your Emotions

I feel angry
I feel frightened
I feel jealous
I feel sad

First published in Great Britain in 1993
by Wayland (Publishers) Ltd

This edition published in 2001 by Hodder Wayland,
an imprint of Hodder Children's Books

© Hodder Wayland 1993

Hodder Children's Books,
a division of Hodder Headline Ltd,
338 Euston Road, London NW1 3BH

Series Editor: Mandy Suhr

British Library Cataloguing in Publication Data
Moses, Brian
 I feel jealous. - (Your Emotions Series)
 I. Title II. Gordon, Mike III. Series
 152.4

ISBN 0-7502-1405-8

Typeset by Wayland (Publishers) Ltd
Printed and bound in Italy by G. Canale & C.S.p.A., Turin

I feel jealous

Written by Brian Moses

Illustrated by Mike Gordon

HODDER
Wayland

an imprint of Hodder Children's Books

When I'm jealous I feel like...
a green-eyed monster
all twisted up inside...

a dog that envies the cat
on his owner's lap.

When I'm jealous...
I sulk in my room,

I won't speak to anyone.

I draw a picture and then scribble all over it.

All sorts of things make me jealous. When my baby sister learns to walk and mum and dad don't seem to notice me...

I feel jealous.

When the boy next door has a new bike...

I feel jealous.

But my bike goes really fast,
even if it isn't new!

When my brother and I play games, he always wins and I feel jealous.

When my best friend goes to tea with someone else I feel jealous.

I say I won't play with her again.

But later I phone and say sorry because I know we all have other friends.

When it's my sister's birthday and there are hundreds of presents, all for her...

I feel jealous.

When my teacher chooses
someone else to feed the fish,
I feel jealous.

But then she chooses me to give out our new books and I like doing that job even more!

When my older brother goes to stay with Gran and Grandad...

I feel jealous.

But Mum says I can have my friend Josie to stay and I know we'll have lots of fun.

When I find myself feeling jealous, it helps if I remember all the good things that I have.

It helps if I can be happy for my friends and enjoy what they have.

It helps if Grandad talks to me.
He seems to know how I feel.

It helps if I think of something special that will happen to me soon.

But sometimes the things I
do might make other children
feel jealous.

If I boast about all my toys...

or how good
I am at swimming.

So next time you feel jealous, remember that sometimes other children may be jealous of you.

Be happy with what you have
and dump those jealous feelings
in the bin!

Notes for parents and teachers

Read the book with children either individually or in groups. Question them about how they feel when they're jealous of somebody or something. Which of the ideas on pages 4-5 are closest to how they feel, or do they picture their jealous feelings in different ways? Can these be illustrated?

How do children behave when they're jealous? Help them to compose short poems where each line begins, 'When I feel jealous...'

> When I feel jealous, there's no one I want to play with.
> When I feel jealous, none of my toys is right for me.
> When I feel jealous...

Ask children whether they think that adults experience feelings of jealousy too.

Much of the book deals with situations that make children feel jealous. Ask them to add to these if they can. Children, of course, will often not realize that feelings of anger and frustration are masks for their jealousy. It may be interesting to ask children to actually make masks that show jealousy and then to discuss the expressions that they have depicted. Whose mask has really succeeded in capturing the feeling in a visual way?

Some children may enjoy writing stories that focus on an aspect of jealousy. They may like to explore one of the situations on pages 6-20 - 'It's not fair, I want a new bike...', 'Why can't I stay with Gran and Grandad?' etc. Will the outcome be positive or negative? Older children may like to write two different endings to their stories showing how the problem is resolved in both ways.

Discuss how our own behaviour affects others. Ask children to talk or write about the things that they might do which make others jealous. Are there ways in which their own behaviour might change to avoid this effect on others?

Explore the notion of jealousy further through the sharing of picture books mentioned in the book list.

The above ideas will help to satisfy a number of attainment targets in the National Curriculum Guidelines for English at Key Stage 1.

FALKIRK COUNCIL
LIBRARY SUPPORT
FOR SCHOOLS

Books to read

Rosie's Babies by Martin Waddell/Penny Dale (Walker Books). Four year old Rosie is just a little jealous of the new baby who seems to have all Mum's attention at the moment.

That's Mine, That's Yours by Angie Sage and Chris Sage (Picture Puffin). Babies want to play with everything that isn't theirs. Big brother finds a way of coming to terms with this.

It's Not Fair! by Bel Mooney (Methuen). Notions of unfairness and the jealous feelings they can engender form the basis for this collection of short stories.

Katie Morag and the Two Grandmothers by Mairi Hedderwick (Picture Lions). Even adults exhibit feelings of jealousy.

The Best of Aesop's Fables by Margaret Clark and Charlotte Voake (Walker Books). See 'The Dog and the Bone'.